Keeping Christmas

Keeping Christmas

Stories to Warm Your Heart Throughout the Year

Compiled and Edited by Barbara Chesser

TAPESTRY PRESS
IRVING, TEXAS

Tapestry Press
3649 Conflans Road
Suite 103
Irving, TX 75061
972 399-8856
info@tapestrypressinc.com
www.tapestrypressinc.com

Printed in Canada

05 04 03 02 2 3 4

Library of Congress Cataloging-in-Publication Data
    Keeping Christmas : stories to warm your heart
throughout the year /
    compiled and edited by Barbara Chesser.
        p. cm.
    ISBN 1-930819-18-8 (alk. paper)
    1. Christmas stories, American. I. Chesser, Barbara.
    PS648.C45 K44 2002
    813'.0108334—dc21
                                    2002009601

Order discounts are available on this and other
Tapestry Press Books. For premium resale or
custom editions, contact Tapestry Press at the
address or telephone number above.

Cover by David Sims

Book design and layout by
D. & F. Scott Publishing, Inc.
N. Richland Hills, Texas

I will honor Christmas in my heart and try to keep it all the year.

Charles Dickens

Contents

Foreword   ix

1   The Miracle of the New Suit   1
     H. Bradford Ramsey, Sr.

2   Choosing To Love   7
     God's Little Daily Devotional

3   The Polished Rock   9
     Linda DeMers Hummel

4   Double Blessing   13
     Victor M. Parachin

5   A Mother's Love   17
     Marijoyce Porcelli

6   The Tablecloth   21
     Richard Bauman

7   Beautiful Day, Isn't It?   25
     As retold by Barbara Johnson

8   A Christmas to Remember   27
     Lewis Grizzard

9   The Carol That Stopped a War   31
     Victor M. Parachin

10 The Hill   35
     Betty J. Reid

11 Christmas Lost and Found   37
     Shirley Barksdale

12 Santa Loves Me, This I Know   43
     Penny Porter

13 The Goodest Gift   49
     Jenna Day

14 Happy Hanukkah and Merry Christmas   55
    Leo Buscaglia

15 An Old Flour Sifter   65
    Lee Hill-Nelson

16 Dancing Rainbows   67
    Vicki Marsh Kabat

17 I Remember Melvin   71
    John T. Baker

18 Ho Ho Hobo   77
    Lee Pitts

19 The Black Sheep Twice Blessed   81
    B. C. Groves

20 The Gift That Kept on Giving   85
    Arleta Richardson

21 Merry Christmas, My Friend   91
    Christa Holder Ocker

22 Santa's Secret   95
    Woody McKay, Jr.

23 The Christmas Nandina   99
    Elizabeth Silance Ballard

24 Celebrating Ben   105
    Andrea Warren

25 Hold Christmas Fast   111
    John C. Bonser

26 A Light in the Window   113
    As retold by Barbara Chesser

A Special Invitation   116

About Barbara Chesser   117

Foreword

All holidays bring back memories, but Christmas rekindles for many people the most vivid memories and evokes the strongest emotions of them all. So much is expected; we all long for the perfect holiday as the year ends and a new one begins. To savor the peace and joy of the season, we must reconcile the disappointments, the tragedies, of the past year—indeed, our entire lifetime—as well as the triumphs, large and small. This collection of heartwarming stories reminds us that while we may have much to mourn, we have more to celebrate!

In whatever ways and rituals you celebrate, may you enjoy these Yuletide stories and may they enrich your life as you recall treasured remembrances and anticipate what is yet to come. Just like the storytellers, may your life be warmed by the wisdom of the season as this wish is granted to you:

A Christmas Wish—
May you never forget what is worth remembering
or never remember what is best forgotten.

An Irish proverb

The Miracle of the New Suit

Where there is great love there are always miracles.
Willa Cather

The first miracle in my life happened at Christmastime, about seventy-five years ago, and that event would be my seed-faith for other miracles yet to come. I was eight when my brother, Orville, and I were invited to attend a banquet for all the newsboys in Birmingham. The affair was sponsored by the newspapers and leaders of the city.

We sold the *Birmingham News*. Orville's corner was at Five-Points, and I hawked papers in front of the Tutwiler Hotel, the grandest hotel I had ever seen. Sometimes on cold evenings the uniformed doorman allowed me to slip into the plush lobby and soak up some warmth. I would bend over and warm my hands in the deep, soft carpet. Then I would gaze with open-mouthed awe at the glittering chandelier and winding marble stairway.

I shall never forget the evening I climbed that marble stairway and entered that elaborate banquet hall. When I took my seat at the table, a handsome, well-dressed young man said he was my sponsor. I was ready to tackle the dessert when my sponsor laid the question on me. "What do you want for Christmas?" he asked.

I was speechless. "Never accept gifts from strangers," Papa always said, and this man sure wasn't an old friend of the family.

"Don't want nothin'," I stammered and wished for Orville. He was two years my senior and was forever bossing me around, like telling me what to say and what not to say. Now, when I needed him, he was at another table across the room.

My sponsor was stunned. "I never saw a boy that didn't want something for Christmas!" he said. After some urging I said, "Aw, jes' get me a bag of marbles!"

Sitting motionless, my sponsor looked straight ahead like he was in shock.

Guess he can't afford a bag of marbles, I decided.

Suddenly he caught me by the chin, and forced me to look him in the eye. "How would you like a new suit of clothes?" he asked.

I was the youngest of four sons of a preacher. The term "new suit of clothes" wasn't in my vocabulary. Our family had a hand-me-down system that left me in full supply of garments Mama had ripped out, sewed up, and rebuttoned. Mama was an expert patcher.

I choked on a chunk of doubt. But when I saw tears on my sponsor's cheeks, I knew he was for real. "Hey, kid! I was a newsboy myself one time!" he said.

Horns tooted, kids laughed, and dishes clattered, but I heard only my sponsor's voice when he said: "Now, I'll ask you again. How about a new suit of clothes for Christmas?"

"That'll be great!" I said.

"You'll get it Christmas Eve," he promised.

Orville and I walked home with our heads in the clouds. He had also been promised a new suit from his sponsor. My miracle began to germinate a few days later. Orville and I, on our way to pick up our newspapers, passed Pizitz department store. There in a display window were two fancy suits for boys.

"Hey Orville!" I yelled, "There's my suit." I pointed to a salt-and-pepper tweed. "That's the one I'm gonna get for Christmas."

"I like the brown one," Orville said.

When I puzzled on how to get word to our sponsors that we had found the suits we wanted, Orville said, "I guess we'll have to pray about it like Papa does when he wants something to happen."

Each night until Christmas Eve I asked God for that suit. In every prayer, I reminded God the suit was at Pizitz department store.

On Christmas Eve a deliveryman brought two packages to our home—one marked for Orville and one for me. We unwrapped our packages while our entire clan watched.

When I opened my box, I felt queasy. It held a beautiful brown suit—the one Orville said he wanted. Orville held up his gift, and I began to cry. *He was holding the suit I had prayed for.* We checked the tags, but there was no mistaking. We each had the suit that had been sent to us.

When I complained, Mama said, "You'd better thank the Good Lord you even got a suit! Now both of you go try your suits on and let's see how they fit."

Orville tried on his jacket and snorted in disgust. "Some dummy sent me the wrong size," he said. I slipped into my coat—the sleeves hung down so far I couldn't see my fingertips. Everyone laughed when we, ill-fitted and disgusted, presented ourselves to our family. "Well," Mama said, "I think you would look better if you traded suits." We did. Orville got the brown suit, and I got the perfectly fitting salt-and-pepper tweed suit.

If only one sugar pie was left, Orville got most of it before the plate reached me. He could talk me out of my warm spot in the bed on cold nights. He was always ahead of me. But, even though he tried it on for size, I got the exact suit I prayed for.

I never asked anyone to explain how two men none of us saw after the Tutwiler banquet found the exact suits two boys wanted, how the suits arrived at the same time, in the wrong size, but ended up on the right boy.

H. Bradford Ramsey, Sr.

H. Bradford "Brad" Ramsey, Sr., former pastor-evangelist, now stays busy as a motivational speaker and storyteller. He has produced four audio-tapes of his Inspirational-Americana series and three books. His new book, How to Claim the Abundant Life With Action Attitudes, *will be released December 2002. He can be reached at P. O. Box 1938, Waco, Texas 76703.*

Choosing To Love

*Love endures long and is patient and kind . . . it takes
no account of the evil done to it . . . pays no attention
to a suffered wrong.*

1 Corinthians 13:4, 5

On Christmas morning, little Amy was delighted
to find a beautiful golden-haired doll among
the presents she unwrapped. "She's so pretty!"
Amy squealed in excitement as she hugged her new doll.
Then, rushing to hug her grandmother, the giver of the
doll, she cried, "Thank you, thank you, thank you!"

Amy played with her new doll most of the day, but toward
evening she put it down and sought out one of her old
dolls. Amy cradled the tattered and dilapidated old doll in
her arms. Its hair had nearly worn away, its nose was broken, one eye was askew, and an arm was missing.

"Well, well," Grandma noted, "it seems as though you like that old dolly better."

"I like the beautiful doll you gave me, Grandma," little Amy explained, "but I love this old doll more, because if I didn't love her, no one else would."

Excerpt taken from
God's Little Daily Devotional
Published by Honor Books
Used by permission.
All rights reserved.

3

The Polished Rock

A great love goes here with a little gift.
Theocritus

He entered my life twenty years ago, leaning against the doorjamb of Room 202, where I taught fifth grade. He wore sneakers three sizes too large and checkered pants ripped at the knee.

Daniel made this undistinguished entrance in the school of a quaint lakeside village known for its old money, white colonial homes, and brass mailboxes. He told us his last school had been in a neighboring county. "We were pickin' fruit," he said matter-of-factly.

I suspected this friendly, scruffy, smiling boy from an immigrant family had no idea he had been thrown into a den of fifth-grade lions who had never before seen torn pants. If he noticed snickering, he didn't let on. There was no chip on his shoulder.

Twenty-five children eyed Daniel suspiciously until the kickball game that afternoon. Then he led off the first inning with a home run. With it came a bit of respect from the wardrobe critics of Room 202.

Next was Charles' turn. Charles was the least athletic, most overweight child in the history of fifth grade. After his second strike, amid the rolled eyes and groans of the class, Daniel edged up and spoke quietly to Charles' dejected back. "Forget them, kid. You can do it."

Charles warmed, smiled, stood taller, and promptly struck out anyway. But at that precise moment, defying the social order of this jungle he had entered, Daniel gently began to change things—and us.

By autumn's end, we all had gravitated toward him. He taught us all kinds of lessons. How to call a wild turkey. How to tell whether fruit is ripe before that first bite. How to treat others, even Charles. Especially Charles. He never did use our names, calling me "Miss" and the students "kid."

The day before Christmas vacation, the students always brought gifts for the teacher. It was a ritual—opening each department-store box, surveying the expensive perfume or scarf or leather wallet, and thanking the child.

That afternoon, Daniel walked to my desk and bent close to my ear. "Our packing boxes came out last night," he said without emotion. "We're leavin' tomorrow."

As I grasped the news, my eyes filled with tears. He countered the awkward silence by telling me about the move. Then, as I regained my composure, he pulled a gray rock from his pocket. Deliberately and with great style, he pushed it gently across my desk.

I sensed that this was something remarkable, but all my practice with perfume and silk had left me pitifully unprepared to respond. "It's for you," he said, fixing his eyes on mine. "I polished it up special."

I've never forgotten that moment.

Years have passed since then. Each Christmas my daughter asks me to tell this story. It always begins after she picks up the small polished rock that sits on my desk. Then she nestles herself in my lap and I begin. The first words of the story never vary. "The last time I ever saw Daniel, he gave me this rock as a gift and told me about his boxes. That was a long time ago even before you were born.

"He's a grown-up now," I finish. Together we wonder where he is and what he has become.

"Someone good, I bet," my daughter says. Then she adds, "Do the end of the story."

I know what she wants to hear—the lesson of love and caring learned by a teacher from a boy with nothing—and everything—to give. A boy who lived out of boxes. I touch the rock, remembering.

"Hi, kid," I say softly. "This is Miss. I hope you no longer need the packing boxes. And Merry Christmas, wherever you are."

Linda DeMers Hummel

Linda DeMers Hummel has been writing profession-ally for twenty years. The mother of three children who are now in college, she has written extensively on the subjects of motherhood and education. She continues to write and teach part-time at Johns Hopkins University. She lives in Baltimore with her dog, Buddha, and three grumpy cats.

Double Blessing

Let us not become weary in doing good, for at the proper time we will reap a harvest.

Galatians 6:9

It was Christmas Eve, 1940, and Eve Gordon was a special-duty nurse at a London hospital. She had been assigned to care for a desperately ill German student from a nearby college. Staff physicians held out little hope for the young man's survival, for he had contracted pneumonia and was in critical condition. The student, aware of his perilous circumstances, pleaded with the nurse to keep him awake, saying, "If I go to sleep, I'll never wake up."

Throughout the long hours of the night, Nurse Gordon kept her patient from drifting off into sleep. With painstaking detail she told him the biblical Christmas story—the journey to Bethlehem, the birth in a stable, the adoration of the shepherds, the visit of the Magi, the flight into Egypt. When she had exhausted the story, she sang to him every Christmas carol she could recall from memory. And whenever her patient seemed on the verge of falling asleep, she gently shook him back to consciousness.

The dawn of that Christmas morning found the student still alive and able to celebrate the day. The crisis passed, and the young man gradually improved and was released from the hospital.

Several years passed. Britain and much of the rest of the world were engulfed in World War II. Gordon, now a medical doctor, had been conscripted into the service of her country. Because she was fluent in Norwegian and a skilled skier, she was placed undercover in Nazi-occupied Norway.

One morning, German occupation troops arrested her along with scores of Norwegian civilians. Someone had tipped off the Germans that one of that group was a British secret agent. Knowing that her true identity and mission would be discovered, Dr. Gordon prayed that death would come quickly and that she would not be subjected to torture.

Brutally shoved into a small room, Dr. Gordon faced her interrogator, a Nazi soldier. The man reached for his side arm. *My prayer is answered*, she thought. Then their eyes met, and there was surprise at the mutual recognition. The German student and the English nurse were face to face again. Replacing his gun in its holster, the soldier pointed to the back door and said: "Go. I give you back your Christmas."

Victor M. Parachin

Victor M. Parachin is an ordained minister. He has served churches in the Chicago, Washington, D.C., and Los Angeles areas. He is a freelance writer and author of several books. He lives in Tulsa, Oklahoma, with his wife and three children.

A Mother's Love

It is more blessed to give than to receive.

Acts 20:35

During the holidays, I sometimes think of Ol' Art. That wasn't his real name. It's just what we fifth-graders called the scrawny, likable classmate with the goofy smile, threadbare pants, and poorly mended shirts.

Not that Ol' Art's poverty meant much in our rural Georgia area. Few people had money, but most had gardens, a pig for yearly meat, and a willingness to share. The problem was Ol' Art's mom. She saw such offers as charity and stoutly refused any aid.

Still, Ol' Art never complained about carrying buttered biscuits for lunch, cheerfully washing them down with water from the hall fountain. The only time Ol' Art thought about his poor state was after suffering a bout of

Lila's taunts. Lila, a local grocer's daughter, jeered at us all, but she seemed to take special pleasure in tormenting Ol' Art. She was in rare form when Ol' Art drew my name for the fifth-grade gift exchange during the upcoming school Christmas party.

"You won't even get a used head scarf this year!" Lila crowed, referring to a hand-me-down I received the previous year at the school's annual gathering. "Ol' Art here couldn't afford a box of dirt."

Ol' Art blushed beet red to the tips of his hair. He blinked fast and crossed his arms tightly against his thin chest, using his bony hand to try to cover the new hole in his shirt sleeve. Feeling awkward and ashamed ourselves, we all looked the other way. I wanted to comfort Ol' Art by reminding him it was Christmas, not presents, that mattered. However, I was a clumsy ten-year-old, too shy to say something so intimate to a boy.

Ol' Art's gift, wrapped in pieces of toilet tissue held together by a piece of twine, heightened Lila's mean giggles. However, she stopped midlaugh, her eyes growing wider than my own, when I pulled from that wad of tissue a sparkling rhinestone bracelet with a gold-plated heart attached. Hanging in the middle of the heart, a miniature gold cross was embedded with a red stone. It was, at that point, the most beautiful thing I had ever seen. I had never dared then to hope for such a possession, even in my dreams.

In fact, like the vagaries of a dream, something familiar tried to tug at my psyche as I stared at the bracelet, but the mental image would not come clear in my state of surprised pleasure. Slightly dazed, I glanced up to see that even the teacher was staring in open-mouthed wonderment at Ol' Art. He was smiling so hard in return it seemed as if his face might soon split with the effort. His happy grin lasted that entire afternoon. When Ol' Art's mom came to walk him home later, her usually grim expression softened at the sight of Ol' Art, and, going out side by side, a slight bounce in her step implied she shared her son's ecstasy.

His mom died the following year, and Ol' Art was taken in by relatives in another state. We never saw him again, but I never forgot him or that bracelet. It was eons later, after years of adulthood, that I ran across that bracelet again. The rhinestones had blackened with age, and the gold-plated heart was scratched and worn; but when I polished the bracelet, the red stone embedded in the miniature gold cross still gleamed.

"How," I finally asked after so many years, "did a fifth-grade boy who ate biscuits and water for lunch afford such a gift?"

It was then when an almost-forgotten sense of familiarity from the past became clear. About a month before that same Christmas party, I was in the school bathroom when I overheard a teacher outside the door ask the woman who had been hired to scrub floors for that day if she wouldn't like to take off her bracelet before beginning.

"I don't take it off until I absolutely have to," the woman had replied, almost apologetically. "My husband gave it to me before he died. I found out later that he had sold his father's watch to get the money to buy it. I don't usually take off this bracelet for any length of time without good reason."

Making this mental connection at last, I realized Ol' Art's mom had eventually felt a compelling enough reason not only to remove her bracelet, but to give it up for good. That reason had been a mother's love. That love was so strong she wanted her son, the poorest boy in that class, to have one shining moment of glory when he was able to give the best gift at the school Christmas party.

Marijoyce Porcelli
Reprinted from *Chicken Soup for the Country Soul*

Marijoyce Porcelli, a freelance writer, has also written for US Airways Magazine, Grit, Orange Coast, Toastmasters, *and many other publications. She teaches creative writing via adult education courses and has finished a book titled* It's All Relatives, *a "slice of humorous family life" about a few eccentric relatives and growing up southern in rural Georgia. She can be reached by E-mail at marijoyce77@ yahoo.com.*

6

The Tablecloth

God moves in a mysterious way.
William Cowper

A young minister had been called to serve at an old church that at one time had been a magnificent edifice in a wealthy part of town. The area and the church, however, were both in a state of decline. Nevertheless, when the minister took charge of the church early in October 1948, he and his wife were thrilled and believed they could restore the church to its former grandeur.

The couple immediately went to work painting, repairing, and attempting to restore the church. Their goal was to have it looking its best for Christmas Eve services.

Just two days before Christmas, however, a driving rainstorm swept through the area. The roof of the old church leaked just behind the altar. The plaster soaked up the rain and then crumbled, leaving a gaping hole in the wall.

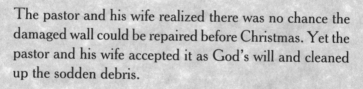

The pastor and his wife realized there was no chance the damaged wall could be repaired before Christmas. Yet the pastor and his wife accepted it as God's will and cleaned up the sodden debris.

The depressed couple attended a benefit auction that afternoon. One of the items put up for bid was an old gold-and-ivory-colored lace tablecloth, nearly fifteen feet long.

Seized with inspiration, the pastor was high bidder at $6.50. His idea was to hang the ornate cloth behind the altar to cover the damaged wall.

On the day before Christmas, snowflakes mingled with the howling wind. As the pastor unlocked the church, he noticed an older woman standing at the nearby bus stop. Knowing the bus wouldn't be there for at least a half-hour, he invited her inside to keep warm.

She wasn't from the neighborhood, she explained. She had been in the area seeking a job as governess to the children of a well-known wealthy family. She was a war refugee, her English was poor, and she didn't get the job.

Head bowed in prayer, she sat in a pew near the back of the church. The pastor was hanging the tablecloth across the unsightly hole when the woman looked up, saw the cloth, and rushed to the altar.

"It's mine!" she exclaimed. "It's my banquet cloth!"

Excitedly she told the surprised minister its history and showed him her initials embroidered in one corner.

She and her husband had lived in Vienna, Austria, and had opposed the Nazis before World War II. They decided to flee to Switzerland, but her husband said they must go separately. She left first. Later she heard that he had died in a concentration camp.

Touched by her story, the minister insisted she take the cloth. She said no, she didn't need it and it looked pretty hanging behind the altar. Then she said goodbye and left.

In the candlelight of the Christmas Eve services, the tablecloth looked brilliant. The white lace seemed dazzling in the flickering light of the candles, and the golden threads woven through it were like dazzling rays of a new dawn.

As members of the congregation left the church, they complimented the pastor on the services and how beautiful the church looked.

One older gentleman lingered, admiring the tablecloth, and as he was leaving said to the minister, "It's strange. Many years ago my wife—God rest her—and I owned such a tablecloth. She used it only on very special occasions. But we lived in Vienna then."

The night air was freezing, but the cold air didn't cause the pastor's goose bumps. As calmly as possible, he told the man about the woman who had been to the church that very afternoon.

"Can it be," gasped the old man, tears streaming down his cheeks, "that she is alive? How can I find her?"

The pastor remembered the name of the family who had interviewed the woman. He telephoned the family and learned her address.

In the pastor's old car they drove to her home on the other side of town. Together they knocked on her apartment door. When she opened it, the pastor witnessed the tearful, joyful, and thrilling reunion of husband and wife.

Some people would call it an amazing coincidence. But the circumstances were far too complex for it to have been mere "coincidence." If one link in the fragile chain of events had been broken, the husband and wife might never have found each other. If the rain hadn't come, if the church roof hadn't leaked, if the pastor hadn't gone to the auction, if the woman hadn't been looking for a job or standing on that corner at just the right time . . . The list of ifs is virtually endless.

It was simply God's will. And, as it has been said many times, He works in mysterious ways.

Richard Bauman

Richard Bauman is a writer whose articles have appeared in over 300 different major publications, including Chicken Soup for the Christian Soul. *He is author of the book* Awe-Full Moments: Spirituality in the Commonplace. *He and his wife, Donna, have been married over forty years. You can contact him at rjb1207@yahoo.com.*

Beautiful Day, Isn't It?

Worse than not having sight is having no vision.
Helen Keller

The day started out rotten. I overslept and was late for work. Everything that happened at the office contributed to my nervous frenzy. By the time I reached the bus stop for my homeward trip, my stomach was one big knot.

As usual, the bus was late—and jammed with holiday shoppers. I had to stand in the aisle. As the lurching vehicle pulled me in all directions, my gloom deepened.

Then I heard a voice from up front boom, "Beautiful day, isn't it?" Because of the crowd, I could not see the man, but I could hear him as he continued to comment on the scenery, calling attention to each approaching landmark. This church. That park. This cemetery. That firehouse. Soon all the passengers were gazing out the windows. The man's enthusiasm was so contagious. I found myself smiling for the first time that day.

We reached my stop. Maneuvering toward the door, I got a look at our "guide": an older figure, wearing dark glasses and carrying a thin white cane.

As retold by Barbara Johnson

Barbara Johnson lives in La Habra, California with her husband, Bill. They have four sons (two deceased). Several bestsellers include Stick a Geranium in Your Hat and Be Happy, Splashes of Joy in the Cesspools of Life, *and* Plant a Geranium in Your Cranium. *Barbara speaks to numerous audiences every year and is the founder of Spatula Ministries.*

A Christmas to Remember

Every man is entitled to be valued by his best moments.

Ralph Waldo Emerson

We had only one real Christmas together, my mother, my father, and I. Only one Christmas when we were actually in our own house with a tree, coffee and cake left out for Santa, and an excited five-year-old awakening to a pair of plastic cowboy pistols, a straw cowboy hat, and an autographed picture of Hopalong Cassidy.

I was heavy into cowboys when I was five. A man never forgets when he scores big at a Western Christmas.

My first Christmas I was only a couple of months old; that doesn't count as a real Christmas together, though, because we were traveling around for a couple of years. The army does that to you.

Then there was Korea. My father went off to war and was captured, but then he escaped, and then we had that one Christmas together before whatever demons he brought back from the war sent him roaming for good.

We were living in Columbus, Georgia, at the time. My father was stationed in Fort Benning, which had been my birthplace. We lived in a tiny frame house with a screen door that had a flamingo in the middle of it. You remember those doors. They were big in the 1950s.

My father, despite what was going on inside him, was a man who found laughter easy, who provoked it from others at every chance, a man easily moved to sentimental tears.

The year after he came back from Korea I used to climb into his lap and feel the back of his head. There were always lumps on the back of his head. "What's these lumps, Daddy?" I would ask.

"Shrapnel," he would answer.

"What's shrapnel?"

He would attempt to explain. It all sounded rather exciting and heroic to a five-year-old boy. My father never complained about the pain, but my mother said he used to get awful headaches, and maybe that's why he couldn't get off the booze.

That one and only Christmas together, my father had duty until noon on Christmas Eve. I waited for him at the screen door, sitting and staring until that blue Hudson—"the Blue Goose"—as my father called it, pulled into the driveway. I ran out and jumped into his arms.

"Ready for Santa?" he asked.

"I've been ready since August," I shouted.

But before we could settle in for our Christmas, my father had to take care of a problem. He had found this family—the man out of work, in need of a shave and a haircut, and his wife crying because her babies were hungry. My father, whatever else he was, was a giving man. He couldn't stand to have when others didn't.

"They're flat on their butts and it's Christmas," I remember him saying to my mother. "Nobody deserves that."

So he somehow found a barber willing to leave home on Christmas Eve, and he took the old man in for a shave and a haircut. Then he bought the family groceries. Sacks and sacks of groceries. He bought toys for the kids, of which there was a house full.

We didn't leave them until dusk. The old man and the woman thanked us, and the kids watched us with wondering eyes. As we drove away in "the Blue Goose," my father broke down and cried. My mother cried, too. I cried because they were crying.

We all slept together that night and cried ourselves to sleep. Next morning, I had my pistols and my hat and my picture of Hopalong Cassidy.

Maybe the three of us had only one real Christmas together—my father had left by the time the next one rolled around—but it was a Christmas a man can carry around in his holster for a lifetime.

Lewis Grizzard

Lewis Grizzard (1947-1994) was described by the national press as "this generation's Mark Twain," "one of the foremost humorists in the country," and "a Faulkner for plain folks." Without a doubt, Grizzard was a masterful storyteller, syndicated columnist, and best-selling author. For more information, contact www.LewisGrizzard.com.

9

The Carol That Stopped a War

Stille nacht, Heilige nacht! Silent night, Holy night!

When World War I erupted in 1914 launching the first great European war of the twentieth century, soldiers on both sides were assured they would be home by Christmas to celebrate victory. That prediction proved to be false. The men on the fronts did not get home for Christmas, as the war dragged on for four years. During that time 8,500,000 men were killed, with hundreds of thousands more dying from injuries. The "war to end all wars" took a horrific human toll and transformed Europe.

However, on Christmas Eve in 1914, one of the most unusual events in military history took place on the Western front. On the night of December 24, the weather abruptly became cold, freezing the water and slush in the trenches in which the men were bunkered. On the German side, soldiers began lighting candles. British sentries reported to commanding officers there appeared to be small lights, raised on poles or bayonets. Although these lanterns clearly illuminated German troops, making them vulnerable to being shot, the British held their fire. Even more amazing, British officers saw, through binoculars, that some enemy troops were holding Christmas trees over their heads with lighted candles in their branches. The message was clear: Germans, who celebrated Christmas on the eve of December 24, were extending holiday greetings to their enemies.

Within moments of that sighting, the British then began hearing a few German soldiers singing a Christmas carol. It was soon picked up all along the German line as other soldiers joined in harmonizing. The words heard were these: "Stille nacht! Heilige nacht!" British troops immediately recognized the melody as "Silent Night, Holy Night" and began singing in English, along with the Germans.

The singing of "Silent Night" quickly neutralized all hostilities on both sides. One by one, British and German soldiers began laying down their weapons to venture into "no man's land," a small patch of bombed out earth between the two sides. So many soldiers on both sides ventured out that superior officers were prevented from objecting. An undeclared truce had erupted and peace had broken out. Frank Richards was an eyewitness of this unofficial truce. In his wartime diary he wrote: "We stuck up a board with 'Merry Christmas' on it. The enemy stuck up a similar one. Two of our men threw their equipment off and jumped on the parapet with their hands above their heads as two of the Germans did the same, our two going to meet them. They shook hands and then we all got out of the trench and so did the Germans." Richards also explained that some German soldiers spoke perfect English, with one saying how fed up he was with the war and how he would be glad when it was all over. His British counterpart agreed.

That night, former enemy soldiers sat around a common campfire. They exchanged small gifts from their meager belongings—chocolate bars, buttons, badges, and small tins of processed beef. Men who only hours earlier had been shooting to kill were now sharing Christmas festivities and showing each other family snapshots. The truce ended just as it had begun, by mutual agreement. Captain C.I. Stockwell, of the royal Welsh Fusiliers, recalled how, after a truly "Silent Night," he fired three shots into the air at 8:30 a.m. on December 26 and then stepped up onto the trench bank. A German officer, who had exchanged gifts with Captain Stockwell the previous night, also appeared on a trench bank. They bowed, saluted, and climbed back into their trenches. A few moments afterwards, Captain Stockwell heard the German officer fire two shots into the air, and the war was on again.

Victor M. Parachin

(See page 15 for biographical data for Victor M. Parachin.)

33

10

The Hill

*You don't stop playing because you are old; you grow
old because you stop playing.*

Bits and Pieces

Long past midnight, hours before dawn,
I jump up from my bed, pull my long johns on.
Peeking out the window, the snow has started to fall.
Slipping on my overalls, I race quickly down the hall.
Rushing to the closet, grasping my old wrap,
I throw it over my shoulder, give the button a snap.
Working all ten fingers through the holes of much-worn
    mitts,
I stick my feet into the boots that thankfully still fit.
Faster than is possible I head straight for the door.
Behind me I am dragging a sled from years before.
The wind is loud and howling, snow is blowing all
    around.
Already what has fallen has covered the ground.
Tramping through the deepness, only my footprints to see,

I head straight for the meadow, the hill is waiting for me.
A few more steps, I reach my goal, as always in the past
I'll be the first to sled this hill, I'll be the very last.
Breathing in the cool night air, I witness the year's first
    snow.
Perhaps this is my favorite spot, in all the sights I know.
Holding tight in a world of silence, I shove off with my
    feet.
Wind is picking up my hair, snow hits against my teeth.
Traveling faster and faster, I struggle not to tip.
Stretching out my snow-damp legs, I lean from hip to hip.
What a big delight, this morn has given thee.
As all years before has done, when it's just this hill and
    me.
Now if I do my best to hurry, I can take another run.
The sun will soon be rising, the day will have begun.
But before that can happen, I must be back in bed
For whatever would the children think . . .
. . . if they knew Grandma used their sled!

Betty J. Reid
Excerpted from *Chicken Soup for the Unsinkable Soul*

*Betty J. Reid resides in Ellicott City, Maryland, with
her husband and son. Besides writing poetry, she
enjoys reading, collecting antiques, and traveling with
family. Her family and friends are often the inspiration behind her poetry. Betty would welcome your
call at 410-461-6951.*

11

Christmas Lost and Found

We shall find peace.
We shall hear the angels.
We shall see the sky
sparkling with diamonds.

Chekov

We called him our Christmas Boy, because he came to us during that season of joy, when he was just six days old. Already his eyes twinkled more brightly than the lights on his first tree.

Later, as our family expanded, he made it clear that only he had the expertise to select and decorate the tree each year. He rushed the season, starting his gift list before we'd even finished the Thanksgiving turkey. He pressed us into singing carols, our croaky voices sounding more froglike than ever compared to his perfect pitch. He stirred us up, led us through a round of merry chaos.

Then, on his twenty-fourth Christmas, he left us as unexpectedly as he had come. A car accident on an icy Denver street, on his way home to his young wife and infant daughter. But first he had stopped by the family home to decorate our tree, a ritual he had never abandoned.

Without his invincible Yuletide spirit, we were like poorly trained dancers, unable to perform after the music had stopped. In our grief, his father and I sold our home, where memories clung to every room. We moved to California, leaving behind our support system of friends and church. All the wrong moves.

It seemed I had come full circle, back to those early years when there had been just my parents and me. Christmas had always been a quiet, hurried affair, unlike the celebrations at my friends' homes, which were lively and peopled with rollicking relatives. I vowed then that someday I'd marry and have six children, and that at Christmas my house would vibrate with energy and love.

I found the man who shared my dream, but we had not reckoned on the surprise of infertility. Undaunted, we applied for adoption, ignoring gloomy prophecies that an adopted child would not be the same as "our own flesh and blood." Even then, hope did not run high; the waiting list was long. But against all odds, within a year he arrived and was ours. Then nature surprised us again, and in rapid succession we added two biological children to the family. Not as many as we had hoped for, but compared to my quiet childhood, three made an entirely satisfactory crowd.

Those friends were right about adopted children not being the same. He wasn't the least like the rest of us. Through his own unique heredity, he brought color into our lives with his gift of music, his irrepressible good cheer, his bossy wit. He made us look and behave better than we were.

In the sixteen years that followed his death, time added chapters to our lives. His widow remarried and had a son; his daughter graduated from high school. His brother married and began his own Christmas traditions in another state. His sister, an artist, seemed fulfilled by her career. His father and I grew old enough to retire, and in Christmas of 1987 we decided to return to Denver. The call home was unclear; we knew only that we yearned for some indefinable connection, for something lost that had to be retrieved before time ran out.

We slid into Denver on the tail end of a blizzard. Blocked highways forced us through the city, past the Civic Center, ablaze with thousands of lights—a scene I was not ready to face. This same trek had been one of our Christmas Boy's favorite holiday traditions. He had been relentless in his insistence that we all pile into the car, its windows fogged over with our warm breath, its tires fighting for a grip on the ice.

I looked away from the lights and fixed my gaze on the distant Rockies, where he had loved to go barreling up the mountainside in search of the perfect tree. Now in the foothills there was his grave—a grave I could not bear to visit.

Once we were settled in the small, boxy house, so different from the family home where we had orchestrated our lives, we hunkered down like two barn swallows who had missed the last migration south. While I stood staring toward the snowcapped mountains one day, I heard the sudden screech of car brakes, then the impatient peal of the doorbell. There stood our granddaughter, and in the gray-green eyes and impudent grin I saw the reflection of our Christmas Boy.

Behind her, lugging a large pine tree, came her mother, stepfather, and nine-year-old half-brother. They swept past us in a flurry of laughter; they uncorked the sparkling cider and toasted our homecoming. Then they decorated the tree and piled gaily-wrapped packages under the boughs.

"You'll recognize the ornaments," said my former daughter-in-law. "They were his. I saved them for you."

"I picked out most of the gifts, Grandma," said the nine-year-old, whom I hardly knew.

When I murmured, in remembered pain, that we hadn't had a tree for, well, sixteen years, our cheeky granddaughter said, "Then it's time to shape up!"

They left in a whirl, shoving one another out the door, but not before asking us to join them the next morning for church, then dinner at their home.

"Oh, we just can't," I began.

"You sure can," ordered our granddaughter, as bossy as her father had been. "I'm singing the solo, and I want to see you there."

"Bring earplugs," advised the nine-year-old.

We had long ago given up the poignant Christmas services, but now, under pressure, we sat rigid in the front pew, fighting back tears.

Then it was solo time. Our granddaughter swished (her father would have swaggered) to center stage, and the magnificent voice soared, clear and true, in perfect pitch. She sang "O Holy Night," which brought back bittersweet memories. In a rare emotional response, the congregation applauded in delight. How her father would have relished the moment!

We had been alerted that there would be a "whole mess of people" for dinner—but thirty-five? Assorted relatives filled every corner of the house; small children, noisy and exuberant, seemed to bounce off the walls. I could not sort out who belonged to whom, but it didn't matter. They all belonged to one another. They took us in, enfolded us in joyous camaraderie. We sang carols in loud, off-key voices, saved only by that amazing soprano.

Sometime after dinner, before the winter sunset, it occurred to me that a true family is not always one's own flesh and blood. It is a climate of the heart. Had it not been for our adopted son, we would not now be surrounded by caring strangers who would help us to hear the music again.

Later, not yet ready to give up the day, our granddaughter asked us to come along with her. "I'll drive," she said.

"There's a place I like to go." She jumped behind the wheel of the car and, with the confidence of a newly licensed driver, zoomed off toward the foothills.

Alongside the headstone rested a small, heart-shaped rock, slightly cracked, painted by our artist daughter. On its weathered surface she had written: "To my brother, with love." Across the crest of the grave lay a holly-bright Christmas wreath. Our number-two son admitted, when asked, that he sent one every year.

In the chilly but somehow comforting silence, we were not prepared for our unpredictable granddaughter's next move. Once more that day her voice, so like her father's, lifted in song, and the mountainside echoed the chorus of "Joy to the World," on and on into infinity.

When the last pure note had faded, I felt, for the first time since our son's death, a sense of peace, of the positive continuity of life, of renewed faith and hope. The real meaning of Christmas had been restored to us. Hallelujah!

Shirley Barksdale

Shirley Barksdale, after the death of her son, used writing as a form of therapy. Since then her writings have appeared in numerous publications including Virtue, Chicken Soup, Reader's Digest, McCall's, and others. She is a member of the Denver Woman's Press Club and resides with her husband in Highlands Ranch, Colorado.

12

Santa Loves Me, This I Know

The moment you have in your heart this extraordinary thing called love and feel the depth, the delight, the ecstasy of it, you will discover that for you the world is transformed.

J. Krishnamurti

One cold Christmas Eve in southeast Arizona, my rancher husband, Bill, arrived home late, as he'd done for forty-five years, after last-minute shopping. Today, using a cane after recent back surgery, he'd searched the mall all afternoon and evening to find the "right" gifts for our family—now numbering fourteen—who would arrive the next day. When he got in at 10:30 p.m., he sank, pale, aching and exhausted into his La-Z-Boy. "I'm getting too old for this kinda stuff," he grumbled.

He had a point. But I had an idea. "How about a whirlpool bath?" I nodded at the monstrous black, plastic tub lurking like a cattle tank at the back of the bathroom. We never used it. And we had reasons.

First, the ominous looking tub was deep, wide and slippery as an oiled salad bowl. It had no grab bars, and every time I dusted it, scorpion skeletons clung to the feather duster like peanut butter to a spoon. Second, I'm a writer, and writers don't like to read directions, especially ridiculous warnings about "how to" turn something on for the first time. So, I'd simply thrown the directions away. After all, a brass button between the spigots said, "PUSH." And I could read, for heaven's sake!

Third, not only was the outside temperature 28 degrees, but our house stood unheated while we awaited furnace parts being shipped from Chicago. Add to these, a twelve-foot-high beamed ceiling, icy tile floors and walls—the bathroom was colder than a slaughterhouse beef locker.

Bill looked at me. "How 'bout I just flatten out under the electric blanket instead?" I sensed a certain plea in his voice.

"But wet heat is supposed to work better." I turned on the spigots, ignoring the steam rising like wood smoke in the icy room. "Besides . . ." I grinned at him. "This tub's plenty big enough for two."

He raised an eyebrow.

A born volunteer, I spoke before I thought, "I'll get in first!" Then I realized it was way too cold to take my clothes off. I glanced at the fireplace beside the tub. No good. Its gas logs were clogged with creosote and I'd forgotten to call the repairman. Only the blue pilot light worked. I saw no way to heat this enormous bathroom on a cold Christmas Eve.

It hit me then. We had five space heaters, huge fifty-pound portable ceramic ovens, complete with coils and blowers. Pulling 220 volts each, they'd warmed newborn foals and calves born on frigid winter nights. These life-saving heaters resided now in our garage, right underneath the fuse box. In a few minutes, I could lug them inside and plug them into sockets currently housing Bill's electric razor and Water Pik, my curling iron, the TV, and various other "not needed at the moment" appliances.

Soon, with extension cords from kitchen to living room, all five heaters were in place. I even turned the electric blanket on HIGH to sustain the tub's aftereffects for Bill. Then I remembered—BUBBLES.

Alas, we were used to showers; Elizabeth Arden and Christian Dior bath salts had no place in our lives. But I did have a substitute—a half-full box of Tide. Better than nothing, I reasoned, aiming the contents beneath the roaring spigots. Before long, the water surface looked like the Alps. I took the first plunge. "Wonderful!" I shouted, unable to see over the mountains of suds. "Come on in, Honey! This'll fix you up in no time." I heard Bill groan as each boot hit the tile floor, but soon I knew that 240 pounds of "love" was displacing an equal volume of H_2O as water rose to my neck. "Are you okay?" I asked.

No answer. Although I couldn't see him, familiar feet grazing my hips accompanied by a deep masculine sigh assured me he was there. The jets would be aimed at his back and his knees. Everything in order, it was time for that magic moment that would make him forget his pain. I didn't *need* directions.

"Ready?" I asked.

"Hmm-hmm."

I pushed the brass button between the spigots.

The roar that followed echoed the finale accompanying the death of the dinosaurs in Walt Disney's *Fantasia*. I felt the undertow—a roiling and churning from the depths of the tub and the bubbles rose higher and higher until— POP—out went the lights! An extraordinary thing happened. In the dim blue glow cast by the fireplace pilot light, I saw Santa rise from the tub:

He was dressed all in bubbles, an unhappy old guy,
And that *wasn't* a twinkle I saw in his eye.
"Penny," he murmured, "don't give me excuses.
You are the one who just blew all the fuses!"
He reached for a towel, and his trusty flashlight,
And I watched my poor Santa drip into the night.

When the power returned and he crawled into bed,
I covered him up and kissed his bald head.
Kids write him, some thank him, and feed his reindeer.
We hug him and kiss him, and love him each year.

But I am the one, when we turned out the light,
Who SLEPT with old Santa that cold Christmas night.

Penny Porter

Penny Porter is a mother and grandmother, former educator, and an award-winning writer of books and articles in Reader's Digest *and other national magazines. Penny often writes of adventures with her family while cattle ranching in Arizona. Her inspiration is rooted in the love of family and human values. Penny can be reached by E-mail at wporter202@ aol.com.*

The Goodest Gift

Good actions are the invisible hinges on the doors of heaven.

Victor Hugo

Every December, as I take out the Christmas decorations, I also take out the memory of a Christmas many years ago, and the gift that one little girl gave to another. In a world where Christmas is ever more glittery and commercialized, it reminds me that the true spirit of the season lies in giving, and receiving, from the heart.

Winters seemed to be colder back then, and school days dragged slowly by. At my small school we had two classes for each grade. My class was for the children who got good grades. Many of the children in the "slower class" were poor, and they didn't seem to get good report cards. By the fourth grade, we all knew who belonged in which class. The one exception was Marlene Crocker.

I still remember the day when Marlene was transferred to the "smarter class." She stood by the teacher's desk that morning wearing ragged clothes and a big, hopeful smile. As she waited for the teacher to assign her a seat, I imagined that she and I might become friends and that we would walk together to recess. Then the whispers began. "She's not sitting beside me!" someone sneered.

"That will be enough," the teacher said firmly. The class was silent. No one would laugh at Marlene again—at least not when the teacher was in the room.

Marlene and I never walked or talked together at recess as I'd first imagined. The boundaries between us seemed too firmly drawn.

One late autumn day, Mom and I were driving along a back road. We were chatting away when suddenly, out the window, I saw a tiny tar-paper shack. It was set far back in a big field littered with rusty car parts. A long clothesline stretched across the yard, and a little girl was hanging out clothes. She looked at us sadly as we sped by. It was Marlene! I raised my hand to wave, but too soon we were gone. "That poor little girl," my mother said, "hanging out clothes when it's going to rain."

Once the snow came that winter, it seemed as though it would never stop. As Christmas drew near, my spirits were as high as the snowdrifts as I watched the pile of presents grow beneath our Christmas tree. At school, we passed a hat around to pick the name of the classmate for whom we'd buy a gift. When the hat came to Marlene, a boy leaned over her shoulder and hooted as he read her slip of paper. "Marlene got Jenna's name!"

I began to blush as I heard my name. Marlene looked down at her desk, but the teasing went on until the teacher stopped it. "I don't care," I vowed haughtily, but I felt cheated.

The day of the party, I marched to the bus reluctantly, carrying a nice store-bought gift of Magic Markers for the person whose name I had drawn. We ate our cookies, and then the wrapping paper went flying as everyone tore into their presents.

The moment I'd been dreading had arrived. It seemed as though everyone was crowding around, looking at the small package, neatly wrapped in tissue paper, on my desk. I looked over at Marlene, sitting alone. Suddenly overcome by the need to protect her from the mocking of our classmates, I seized Marlene's present, unwrapped it and held it, hidden in my hand.

"What is it?" a boy hollered, when he could stand it no longer.

"It's a wallet," I finally answered.

The bell rang and the buses came and someone said to Marlene, "Did your old man make it from the deer he shot?"

Marlene nodded and said, "And my ma."

"Thank you, Marlene," I said.

Marlene and I smiled at each other. She was not my friend, but I never teased her. Maybe when I was older I could ride my bike over to her place. I thought about that as I rode the bus home. I tried not to think of what Marlene's Christmas would be like.

Years went by. I went away to high school and college. Whenever I struggled with math problems, I recalled the way that Marlene had always breezed through hers. I heard that she had left school after the eighth grade to help her mother with the younger children at home.

One day, when going through my things, I came across the white doeskin wallet that I'd received at that Christmas party long ago. As I studied the intricate craftsmanship, I noticed a small slit holding a tiny piece of paper which I hadn't seen before. I unfolded it and read the words that Marlene had written to me years before. "To my best friend," they said. Those words pierced my heart. How I wished that I could go back and have the courage to be the kind of friend that I'd wanted to be. Too late, I understood the love that had been wrapped inside that gift.

A few things I unpack every year at Christmastime—an old wooden crèche, shiny balls for the tree—and the wallet. One year, I told my small son the story of the girl who had given the homemade wallet to me. He thought about it and then he said, "Of all the gifts, that was the goodest gift, wasn't it?"

And I smiled, grateful for the wisdom that let him see that it was.

Jenna Day

Jenna Day is a writer and educator who lives in Fryeburg, Maine. She is a graduate of the University of Southern Maine and is currently working on a graduate degree in Literacy Education. She enjoys bird-watching, sailing, and spending time with her husband, sons, mother, and aunt.

Happy Hanukkah and Merry Christmas

The heart generous and kind most resembles God.
Robert Burns

I could not have been more than eight or nine years old the Christmas our new neighbors moved in. It was an exceptionally cold and rainy Los Angeles December. I remember it well because of the embarrassment I felt over having to wear my sister's winter coat, which she had outgrown. In our home, clothes were not thrown out, they were handed down. And it was my turn—no matter the girlish fur piping on the collar and the sleeves or buttons on the wrong side.

We lived in a small house heated by a single wood-burning stove that separated the kitchen and the dining room. I remember how we huddled that December to dress by its heat. The house was frame, similar to many others still found in the Boyle Heights area of Los Angeles. They were called craftsman houses.

The families who lived on our street were mostly first-generation immigrants: Jews from eastern Europe, Italians from southern Italy, Germans, and Mexicans. Few of them spoke much English, most had large families, all of them were poor.

Our new neighbors arrived in early December—a rabbi and his family: a boy, Elijah, who was my age, and a girl, Sarah, a few years older. When I saw them for the first time, I pretended to be playing, but watched as their large old pieces of furniture were unloaded from the moving van and disappeared into the darkness behind their front door. I wondered what they'd be like, if they'd speak English, if they'd be friendly. As is usually the case under such circumstances, it was Elijah and I who were the first to talk. It always seems easier for children, for some reason. We were soon walking to school each day, fast becoming close friends. He was one of the few children who didn't laugh at my coat.

We were standing in the schoolyard waiting for the bell to ring one morning when the subject of the approaching holiday came up.

"What are you going to get for Christmas?" I asked Elijah.

"I don't believe in Christmas," he said simply.

I was stunned. "Everybody believes in Christmas," I insisted.

"I'm Jewish. We don't," he answered matter-of-factly.

"Well, what do you believe in if you don't believe in Christmas?" I persisted.

"Lots of things. But not Christmas," he responded.

When something of any importance happened during the day in our lives, it was always shared with the family at our dinner table that evening. It was here that anxieties were lessened, mysteries solved, solutions arrived at. I couldn't wait to tell the startling news. Our new neighbors didn't believe in Christmas.

Mama and Papa were as mystified as I was at the news. They were not moved by my elder brother's explanation that Christmas is a religious holiday, that there are all kinds of beliefs in the world, that the Cohens had as much right not to believe in Christmas as we did to believe in it. After all, he reasoned further, wasn't that part of why so many people left their homelands to immigrate to the United States?

Mama in her innocent wisdom rationalized, "Maybe they don't know about it. They come from far away, like we do, and maybe no one told them yet."

"Well, they don't come from the moon," my brother laughed.

"Don't be so smart," my mother said, "or I'll send *you* to the moon!" Mama had a way of making a point. She turned to Papa across the table. "They should be invited to share Christmas with us," she said.

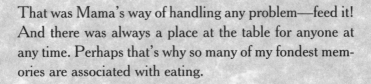

That was Mama's way of handling any problem—feed it! And there was always a place at the table for anyone at any time. Perhaps that's why so many of my fondest memories are associated with eating.

Within a week of their moving in, I was hired by Rabbi Cohen as their *Shabbes goy*: the Gentile who serves the family on their Sabbath. I was paid generously—a nickel a week for the job, a fortune for a poor kid at the time. It was very easy. I just had to turn on the lights when the family returned from the synagogue, move a few pots of food to the stove and turn on the gas.

This, of course, became another mysterious subject for our table talk. "How come you have to do that? That's really strange."

A few weeks prior to Christmas, I was serving the Cohen's Sabbath table. When I finished my ritual, I did as I had been instructed by Papa and invited Rabbi Cohen and his family to Christmas dinner at our home. Elijah had warned me that they wouldn't come.

Rabbi Cohen was a man not easily forgotten. He was of medium stature but appeared much larger than life, with his bespectacled, alert, dark eyes, his shocking mass of black hair, his dark beard and his black clothing—all serving to accentuate the whiteness of his delicate face and hands. We all thought that he was the very image of the man on the Smith Brothers cough drop box.

In his deep, melodious voice he answered my invitation. "Ah," he said, "Ve would like to come to your house and meet your mama and papa, but better I talk first to your papa."

"They don't talk English too good," I warned him. "That's why they asked me to invite you. They talk Italian."

"Vell," the rabbi said with a smile, "I don't talk too good, either. But ve'll understand each other. Vy not? Ve're neighbors."

When he was at home Papa could always be found in his garden. Behind the house grew endless vegetables: onions, peppers, garlic, zucchini, carrots, lettuce and whatever the seasonal vegetables or fruits were. The front of the house was always a profusion of flowers. It was especially lovely this Christmas season, with large bushes of poinsettias— double red, in full bloom.

Rabbi Cohen stopped Papa at his weeding a few days later. Elijah and I, now good friends, stood close by to watch the historic encounter.

"I'm Rabbi Cohen, your new neighbor."

"I know you jus-a move in," Papa said. "Is-a good you jus-a move in."

"It's time ve should meet," Rabbi Cohen said, with his unique inflection. He shook Papa's hand warmly. "I vant to thank you for the invitation to be vis you and your family for Christmas dinner."

"It's-a all right," Papa said. "You and your family come. We gotta plenty to eat."

"That's a problem," the rabbi smiled. "You see, ve can only eat certain style foods. Ve run a kosher household."

"Well," said Papa, in the usual way he had of refusing to allow anything to present a problem. "We'll cook what-a you eat—kosher." Of course, Papa had no idea what kosher was. He was counting on Mama's usual creativity in the kitchen.

"Vell," replied Rabbi Cohen, "it's a little bit more complicated dan dat."

He proceeded to explain what a kosher household entails. Papa nodded understanding, but it became plain that evening at the dinner table that he had understood very little of what the rabbi told him. What he concluded was that Jews ate differently from other people, that they did know what Christmas was all about, and that they too had a very special holiday in December called Hanukkah. But in spite of communication problems, Papa was delighted to tell us that the Cohens would be our guests for Christmas dinner and, in turn, we were invited to share their Hanukkah ceremony several nights later.

My elder sister was sent out to the nearby kosher market on Wabash and Evergreen with instructions to buy enough kosher food to satisfy at least ten people. Papa wanted to be sure there would be enough. Though we had very little money to spare, feeding our new neighbors was a very high priority.

My mother was delighted and intrigued when my sister returned with large bags of assorted foods in tightly sealed jars and containers marked "kosher." The grocer had helped her select a very special feast, indeed.

Both holiday visits were great successes. After surmounting various problems and supplying appropriate utensils of their own, the Cohens were very touched by the special dinner set before them. The Buscaglias devoured their Christmas feast with their accustomed gusto. There were gifts for the Cohens under the Christmas tree, and in the soft glow of Christmas lights we serenaded them with carols, in both English and Italian.

Each year Mama proudly displayed a traditional manger scene which was made up of several small hand-carved figures: Mary, Joseph, the infant Jesus, and a few shepherds, angels, and animals which she had managed to carry with her among the few possessions she brought from Italy. Over the manger was a tiny banner on which were printed the words *"Pace sulla terra agli uomini di buon volonta."*

During the evening Mrs. Cohen fingered each of the images tenderly, then asked, "What does the banner say, Mrs. Buscaglia?"

"Pace. Peace," Mama answered.

"Yes," Rabbi Cohen sighed. "Peace."

I can remember much laughter that night, but I recall more vividly the tears brought on by shared memories of "the old country." How much they missed the families left behind, the dear friends, the special foods now unavailable, the places of their childhood that perhaps they would never see again.

Several evenings later, we sat in the Cohens' living room eating potato *latkes*, sharing small glasses of wine and breaking bread—the *challah*. We watched in silence as Mrs. Cohen lit the last of the Hanukkah candles from the flame of the *shammash*—eight in all—until the menorah was ablaze with light. Mrs. Cohen looked beautiful in the bright candlelight. "Like a Madonna," my mother told her. "Oy vey," Mrs. Cohen said, "a Jewish Madonna!" We listened to the prayers and the songs. Rabbi Cohen had a beautiful bass voice that towered over the others in a strange harmony. We were all presented with Hanukkah gifts. We learned to spin the dreidel, a great game that produced much laughter.

When the time came for us to depart, Rabbi Cohen put his arm around my father's shoulder. "Hanukkah isn't Christmas, but like your Christmas, it's a time of a miracle, a Festival of Light," he explained. He told us it celebrates a rededication of their temple, a reminder to put away thoughts of revenge and battle and share love in peace with family and friends. "Just like it was on your manger—time for 'Peace on earth to men of goodwill.'"

I can still visualize the moment when we departed from the Hanukkah celebration. Papa huddled us all together under umbrellas at the bottom of the Cohens' front porch. He turned and said, "Happy Hanukkah, *cari amici*." Rabbi Cohen, his family surrounding him, smiled down at us, "Merry Christmas, neighbors. *Mazel tov!*"

This was the beginning of a loving friendship between our two families that was to last more than thirty years. Thirty years in which so many things happened, none of which we could foretell during that first special season. Rabbi Cohen died one day on his way to *shul*. His heart simply stopped. My brothers and sisters, one by one, left home. Elijah got married and I was his best man. His sister went off to college to become a doctor. Mrs. Cohen went to live with her brother in New York. My parents sold the family home and moved into a small apartment nearer to my elder sister.

Beautiful memories recalled have a way of re-creating the original glow and warmth surrounding them. I feel them still, writing these thoughts, even after fifty years. I can settle back and yield to the feeling of love we radiated during that holiday, a love that will never die as long as there is one of us to remember.

"Happy Hanukkah, *cari amici*."

"Merry Christmas, neighbor. *Mazel tov!*"

Leo Buscaglia

Leo Buscaglia (1924–1998) was a well-loved author and lecturer on the dynamics of human relations, especially the topic of love. His books have been bestsellers from Japan to Turkey, with five appearing on the American bestseller lists in the 1980s. Used by permission, "Happy Hanukkah and Merry Christmas" originally appeared in Seven Stories of Christmas Love *as "Two Festivals of Light." For information, contact the Felice Foundation at P.O. Box 265, Palos Verdes Estates, CA 90274, or www.buscaglia.com/felice.*

15

An Old Flour Sifter

I am in the habit of looking not so much to the nature of a gift as to the spirit in which it is offered.
Robert Louis Stevenson

 flour sifter, darkened and a bit rusted around the edges, sits in my cabinet amid pots and pans. It will stay there forever.

Christmas came to earth as a child, a gift from God. My mom used to say, "It's not the gift, but who is the giver." I agree.

The sifter was a Christmas gift from my three-year-old daughter. I had come home from the hospital after giving birth to a new baby girl. Our house did not look like Christmas—no gifts, no decorations, nothing baked. Connie wanted to go to the grocery store with her Daddy. She came home with shining eyes, hugged my neck, and handed me a paper sack.

"Your Christmas gift. It's a flour sifter," she said.

I don't know why she chose a flour sifter. I don't remember if I even needed one. But I do know the gift was important to her, and it's a gift I remember—and cherish.

She's grown up now with a family of her own. Recently, I asked her if she remembers the sifter. She thought for a bit and then said, "Oh, yes. We sifted much flour in those days. No cake mixes for us."

The memory is sweet, and it reminds me that Christmas comes to us as a child, a gift from God.

My cup runs over!

Lee Hill-Nelson

Lee Hill-Nelson, retired church secretary, wife, mother, and grandmother, has published numerous personal experience articles and children's stories. She has always lived in Texas except for twenty months service in the U.S. Navy WAVES. Lee is a mentor for boys thirteen to eighteen years of age in reading classes at a youth center.

Dancing Rainbows

*We tend to forget that happiness doesn't come as a
result of getting something we don't have, but rather of
recognizing and appreciating what we do have.*

Frederick Koenig

Christmas is a season of symbols—Santa and
reindeer, mistletoe and fir trees. But there are
two other symbols I think of at Christmas—a
broken heart and dancing rainbows.

It began nine years ago when our family traveled to
Nebraska for what would be our last Christmas with both
my in-laws—everyone called them ViVi and Cuzzy. I can
still see their smiles and excited waves when they saw our
old station wagon pull up to their home.

The few days were fun-filled and boisterous, with all of the
extended family gathered together. The grandchildren
crawled into ViVi's lap for bedtime stories, ran to her for

fresh-baked gingerbread boys and giggled as she sang funny songs.

ViVi was hard to shop for, and I had looked a long time for a Christmas present for her that year. I wanted to give her something that would symbolize what she meant to us. She always put the needs of her husband and children first. She was the heart of our family.

Finally I found what I was searching for—a beautiful, lacy glass heart to hang in the window. ViVi so enjoyed prisms and stained glass hangings that caught the sun's rays. She filled her kitchen with dancing rainbows.

ViVi's face lit up when she unwrapped the glass heart. She gave me a hug and immediately put it in her bedroom window. During the rest of our stay, I often saw her slip back into the bedroom to admire the fragile heart.

Too soon it was time for us to leave. As she always did when we left, ViVi stood on the front stoop and waved goodbye, trying not to let us see her tears.

The months passed quickly after we returned home. Then suddenly, our lives were punctuated by the first of many frightening phone calls. ViVi was in the hospital. She has having trouble with her heart. She would need a triple bypass.

Then, too quickly for us to grasp, she was gone, unable to survive the operation.

Stunned, my husband and his siblings gathered once again in Nebraska. Circumstances prevented the children and me from going. On a cold, misty spring day, they said goodbye to ViVi. Hundreds of miles away, I sat staring out the window in disbelief.

A month later, we all went to Nebraska to spend time with Cuzzy. ViVi's smiling face was not there to greet us this time. Walking into their home, the reality of her loss hit me full force.

Until that visit, I had managed to deny ViVi's death. Now there was no escaping it. Cuzzy wanted me to pack her clothes and costume jewelry. It was a heartbreaking task, and I soon had to step away from it all to collect my thoughts. I went to the window and pulled open the drapes. As sunshine filled the room, I saw something glitter.

At first, I didn't realize what it was. When I did, the tears that had threatened so many times finally spilled over. There on the windowsill were the shattered pieces of the glass heart I had given ViVi for Christmas. Its suction cup had loosened and the heart had broken.

Carefully, I brushed the pieces into my hand. The sun shone through the fragments and sent dancing rays of color into the room.

I stood there for a long time that day. I let the tears fall, and I let my heart grieve. It was an ending, but also a beginning. The heart of this family had not been broken beyond repair, as had the glass heart in my hand. The light of ViVi's love could still cast rainbows into our lives.

Every Christmas Day since, I have slipped away from the piles of toys and the laughing children. I find a quiet place to sit and think about ViVi and broken hearts.

And, once again, I look for the dancing rainbows in my world.

Vicki Marsh Kabat

Vicki Marsh Kabat, a University of Missouri-Columbia journalism graduate, has worked in advertising, newspapers, book publishing, and public relations. Her book, MomSense: For Clueless Parents Everywhere, *is a collection of her humor columns.* Chicken Soup for the Golden Soul *also includes her work. She is editor of* Baylor [University] Magazine. *She and her husband, Bruce, have three sons.*

17

I Remember Melvin

*I assure you that unless you change and become like
children, you will never enter the Kingdom of heaven.*
Matthew 18:3

He was five when I first saw him. I'll never forget. It was Christmas Eve, and I was getting ready to leave the office when Gibney popped her head in.

"Can you see one more patient, Doctor?" she coaxed.

I frowned at my nurse. She knew I had promised Mary to be home early—for a change. We were having guests for the holiday.

Quickly I ran through the checklist.

"Appointment?"

Gibney knew that I knew that all the day's appointments had been completed.

"No, Doctor, but . . ."

"Regular?"

Allowances have to be made for regular customers.

She shook her head.

"Emergency?"

The last loophole.

Gibney hesitated. "I don't think so, Doctor," she said slowly.

I hung up my smock and reached for my jacket. "Tell them to make an appointment. I'm running late."

I picked up my bag and headed for the door. Gibney didn't move—except to fold her arms across her chest. I stopped and sighed. I knew that signal. The veteran nurse was about to admonish the young pediatrician. Once again he was going to be given the benefit of her long years of experience.

I dropped my bag. It would be quicker to see the patient. "All right, Gibney. But make it snappy!"

She didn't exactly smile. More of an approving nod. Teacher had received the right answer. She was back by the time I had my smock on.

"This is Mrs. Duncan, Doctor," she announced, ushering in a large black woman. Confound it, I thought, Gibney's gone off her rocker. This person belongs in obstetrics, or gynecology, or internal medicine—anywhere but pediatrics.

Then I saw my patient, peeping out from behind the voluminous skirt. He was every bit as black, but as skinny as she was fat. Except his stomach. It was distended.

"This is Melvin, Doctor." The woman's voice was like plum pudding. "He's got something wrong."

I took a closer look at the lad. Something wrong, indeed, and not much doubt what it was. I held out my hand. "Hello, Melvin. How do you feel?"

He ducked his head and put his hand in mine. "I feel jus' fine, Doctor," he piped.

How many times over the next five or six years I would hear those exact words! No matter how sick Melvin was, no matter how much pain, whenever I asked, his reply never varied: "I feel jus' fine, Doctor."

As I examined him that first day, Flora Duncan—*Saint Flora*, by all rights, because, as I came to know, she had a heart at least twice as big as her enormous body— explained that Melvin was not a relative, "just a friend."

I later learned both his parents had been killed in an automobile accident a few months previously. No relatives turned up, so Flora Duncan, a neighbor, was looking after him.

And look after him she did, from that day when I told her the diagnosis—sickle cell anemia—and the prognosis—bleak at best—until the very last.

I saw Melvin regularly until he was ten or eleven. His condition slowly but steadily deteriorated. And medical science could do no more than treat the symptoms with painkillers. But he never lost heart. His eyes got bigger in his thin face, but the sparkle was as bright as ever.

Not once did I ever hear him complain, not in the office, not in the hospital, not at home—in those days I still made house calls. His response was always the same: "I feel jus' fine, Doctor."

The way he said it, you almost believed it. Except you knew better. Finally—cerebral hemorrhage.

Gibney and I went to the funeral, the only whites there. We sat with Flora Duncan. The preacher's text was "Be of good cheer." Gibney and I cried.

A few days later—again on Christmas Eve—Flora brought Melvin's sister by the office. The little girl had a gift for me—a small dish crudely fashioned out of clay.

"Melvin wanted you to have this, Doctor," she explained. "He made it the day before he died."

That was many years and many patients ago. But that clay dish is still on my desk. As I look at it every day, and think of all the whining and sniveling going on in this world, I keep hearing Melvin:

"I feel jus' fine, Doctor."

John T. Baker

John T. Baker is a former teacher, government agent, and business executive, now retired, whose poems and stories have appeared in numerous literary journals and on the Internet. He has adapted a number of plays and written lyrics for stage productions and is the co-author of several books on American idiomatic expressions.

18

Ho Ho Hobo

Be not forgetful to entertain strangers: for thereby some have entertained angels unawares.

Hebrews 13:2

'Twas the night before Christmas and the family was en route to Grandma's house. As they motored through the intersection of a small sleepy town, the ill-mannered child in the back seat yelled into his father's ear, "It's him, it's him, it's Santa Claus."

There on the curb was a forlorn-looking fellow with a dirty white beard, a stocking cap that barely covered his head, and a red tattered coat that was frayed white around the edges.

The parents glanced at the ragged man with all his possessions sitting next to him in a plastic grocery bag. "You have to admit," said the mother, "he does look like Santa with his scuffed-up old boots and his matted beard."

"Don't be silly, he's just a ho ho hobo," laughed the father. "The only thing that transient has in common with Santa is he probably only works one day a year."

But the child was throwing a tantrum in the back seat. "I want to stop and see Santa!"

"He looks more like Santa than those photocopies back home," said the mother as the car rolled to a stop and the kid escaped out the back door.

"Hi, Santa," said the child, shocking the jolly old gent out of his quiet reverie. Despite his age the old man was quick to catch on. With the parents looking a bit apprehensive, the old man pulled the young boy up on one knee of his dirty old pants. Before the homeless man realized what was happening, the child was listing the presents he expected to find the very next morning under the Christmas tree.

"I want a joy stick, a bike, and a laser gun." The old man had never heard of many of the toys the boy rattled off. "My sister wants a baby that drinks, wets, and cries. Daddy wants a new table saw and mommy wants a fur coat. But you already know all that because I sent you a letter. You got it didn't you?"

The old man didn't know what to say and just nodded his head. He hadn't spoken to a child or held one on his lap for many years.

"I have to warn you," said the boy to the smiling Santa, "Grandma doesn't have a chimney so we'll have to leave the front door unlocked for you."

The parents looked sick as they shared a vision of this bum walking through an open door and stealing all their presents. "Come on, son, we have to be going now."

"Maybe you better write this down so you don't forget it all," said the son to Santa, ignoring his parents as usual.

Before putting the boy down, the old man reached into his sack for something to give the child, but there was nothing in the sack but dirty clothes. There was a tear in the old man's eye as he reached to his neck and took off a gold chain with a golden cross with the figure of Jesus attached. He had worn the crucifix for as long as he could remember. A reminder of better times. He gave that small boy the only possession he owned that was worth anything. "You keep this present and do what your mom and dad tell you. And whenever you need some extra help in life, you just grab hold of this cross and pray. . ."

The parents looked grateful and sad, and then realized they had a lot of shopping to do before the next morning if they were to acquire all the presents on their child's wish list. They waved goodbye to the old man who lived out of a sack.

Once they were back in the car the young boy told his dad, "That was the best Santa of all."

Years later the youngster had children of his own. At about the age of six, one by one, his kids would ask, "Dad, is there really a Santa Claus?" He would clasp the gold crucifix he wore close to his heart and reply, "Yes, there is. I met him in person."

Lee Pitts

Lee Pitts is executive editor of the Livestock Market Digest _and writes a syndicated weekly column that appears in publications in the U.S. and Canada. His books include_ People Who Live At the End of Dirt Roads _and_ Back Door People. _His essays are regularly recited by Paul Harvey._

19

The Black Sheep Twice Blessed

*Love cannot be forced, love cannot be coaxed and
teased. It comes out of Heaven, unasked and
unsought.*

Pearl Buck

My best friend Jean was five and a half years old when her mother died, leaving her and her little sister. She never liked Christmas after that. Christmas was for families, and Jean simply didn't belong to her father's new family. Her father's wife resented having Jean intrude on the precious moments of what she called her "family's affair." Family meant the wife's four children and Jean's father—but not Jean.

Any gifts Jean received she had to share with the younger children. The family was poor, so sharing was the norm. But it still hurt Jean terribly to have her gifts taken from her and given to the younger children; the sharing all went one way. Throughout Jean's childhood, Christmas became the hated holiday of heartache and hypocrisy instead of the celebration of love.

Jean had one gift from a Christmas past that she hid, one she couldn't bear to share, one she rarely touched. This treasured toy was a stuffed black sheep; it was the last present her mother ever gave her. The black sheep was more than a toy for Jean; it was a cherished symbol of unconditional love. She kept the little black sheep in a special hiding place and took it out only occasionally, not so much to play with, but to look at and to remember. Then one day the eldest child of her father's wife saw the sheep and cried to have it. Her father's wife snatched the toy out of Jean's hand and gave it to her favorite child. She punished Jean, saying she was bad because she didn't want to share.

In no time the little sheep's eyes were gone and then the ears. White cotton stuffing poked out of the broken seams of its head. Jean tried to rescue the toy and to stitch the seams together. But she was punished again for disobeying. The little black sheep was no longer her toy. The last time Jean saw the little black sheep was outside, trampled in the red mud of winter. Soon afterwards, her father's wife threw it in the trash. Jean hid her painful tears over the little black sheep. She was not allowed to show sorrow or happiness—or any emotion at all. But the loss of the little black sheep—and her mother—burrowed deep in her heart and ached for many years afterward. The little black sheep had become a symbol of what Jean had become in her father's home.

For several years after she was grown, Jean would think about the little black sheep when she shopped for Christmas presents for her daughter. It would stand about nine inches high and be covered with a black wooly coat. But it never turned up. Eventually Jean forgot about it. The daughter grew up and gave Jean two beautiful grandsons that she adored.

On a recent Christmas when Jean's grandsons were big enough to understand that Christmas meant love and sharing, they were playing Santa Claus as Jean and the other grandmother sat next to each other in a circle of extended family. The younger grandson, three and a half, heaved a big square box on Jean's knees and waited for her to open it. The contents of the package would be a surprise to him also.

Jean carefully removed the bright colored bow and paper, halfway teasing the young grandson. In the spirit of fun, he eventually tore into the package to help his grandmother open the package. Wrapped in white tissue, there it was—a little stuffed sheep with a wooly coat and bright eyes that shown in the twinkling lights of the Christmas tree.

At first Jean was stunned and couldn't speak. When she tried, tears filled her eyes. Embarrassed, she buried her hands in her face. Without missing a beat, Jean's grandson threw his tiny arms around her and pulled her head to his shoulder. He patted her cheek and said, "It's alright, Bammie. I'll take care of you. Where do you hurt? Do you have an owie?" After a few minutes, Jean was able to smile through her tears and to answer her grandson's heartfelt question.

"Not anymore."

B. C. Groves

B. C. Groves writes about Texas and Texans. A former Texas educator, she is currently working on her second novel, Heroes of Lively County. *She has published several articles in various periodicals, newspapers, and compilations. She hails from Wise County, Texas and now lives with her husband in Oregon.*

20

The Gift That Kept on Giving

The joy that you give others is the joy that comes back to you.

John Greenleaf Whittier

I was searching through Grandma's old trunk when I came across a small, leather-bound book, the edges crumbly and dusty. It was a copy of Snowbound, and "John Greenleaf Whittier" was inscribed on the first page.

"Look, Grandma," I said. "Is this the book you told me about that Sarah Jane signed?"

"No," Grandma replied. She turned the book over lovingly. "This is the original one."

"But you sold that one to Warren Carter."

"I did," Grandma nodded. "The money he gave me helped get a coat with a fur collar for Ma's Christmas."

"But, how——?"

"How does it happen to be here? That's quite a story," Grandma said. "I guess I've never told you more than the first part of it."

"Tell me now," I urged her, and together we went back in time to Mabel's high school years.

Warren Carter did give me five dollars for my autographed copy of *Snowbound*, and I was content with the copy that Sarah Jane had signed to look like the original. Ma enjoyed her coat so much that I never regretted the choice I had made.

Just before we graduated from high school, Warren stopped in to see me one evening.

"Mabel," he said, "you've given me a run for my money ever since we started school together. I think you deserve a graduation gift for making me work."

He handed me a wrapped and ribboned package, and grinned happily as I opened it. It was the copy of *Snowbound* I had sold to him in the eighth grade. "Oh, Warren! Are you sure you want me to have this back?"

He nodded. "It's too valuable a thing for you ever to have sold. You've been a good friend over the years, and I want you to keep it."

One Christmas, when Alma was about eight years old, there was no money for gifts for the family. Sarah Jane and I made doll clothes from scraps for our daughters' dolls.

"What are you doing for Len this year?" Sarah Jane asked as we worked on our sewing.

"I've made him a sweater and socks," I said, "but the truth is, I want to get him a Bible. We have a nice family Bible, and the church Bible, but he needs a reading Bible the size of his hymnal. I could get one from the catalog for seventy-five cents, but the one I really have my eye on is bound in French Morocco and has gold edges."

"How much is it?"

"$1.40. I pick it up and look at it every time I go into Gages' store. Maybe I'll give it so much wear that they'll lower the price."

"Dorcas would let you get it and pay a little at a time," Sarah Jane said.

I shook my head. "Len wouldn't enjoy reading it if he knew I'd gone into debt for it. He would say that a Bible here and one at church is enough. But I know how much he'd like one he could carry with him."

"How much do you still need?"

"Seventy-five cents."

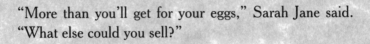

"More than you'll get for your eggs," Sarah Jane said. "What else could you sell?"

"Nothing that I know of." I shrugged. I thought for a moment. "Well, maybe there is. My autographed copy of *Snowbound*."

Sarah Jane was appalled. "Oh, Mabel, no! I was thinking of something to eat, like cream or vegetables. That book is priceless!"

"So is Len," I replied. "I'll take it in to Dorcas and see if she'll buy it. Or at least trade it for the Bible."

The next time I went into town, I took the slender volume and explained my plan to Dorcas Gage.

"Are you sure, Mabel?" she protested. "This book is a treasure. Mr. Whittier is dead now, and there may not be many autographed copies of one of his most famous poems."

"I know. But how often do I read it? Len would read his Bible every day."

Dorcas was reluctant, but she took the book in return for the Bible, and I hurried home, more than pleased with my bargain.

When gifts were opened on Christmas morning, Len was delighted, as I knew he would be. As usual, we shared the day with Thomas and Sarah Jane. As we prepared to leave their home that evening, Sarah Jane handed me a small package.

"One more little gift," she said.

When I opened the present, I very nearly burst into tears. It was my autographed copy of *Snowbound*.

"Who knows what that book might buy next year?" Sarah Jane said with a grin. "I figured this was the best investment you could ever have."

But she was mistaken. Actually, the best investment of my life had been her friendship.

Arleta Richardson

Arleta Richardson began her career as a teacher/ librarian and then started her writing career in 1970. She has published in numerous magazines, devotionals, and authored the successful Grandma's Attic series books published in several languages. She has also authored children's books and has two other books in progress.

21

Merry Christmas, My Friend

Love is the only thing we can carry with us when we go, and it makes the end so easy.

Louisa May Alcott

"I will never forget you," the old man said. A tear rolled down his leathery cheek. "I'm getting old. I can't take care of you anymore."

With his head tilted to one side, Monsieur DuPree watched his master. *"Woof, woof! Woof, woof!"* He wagged his tail back and forth, wondering, *What's he talking about?*

"I can't take care of myself anymore, let alone take care of you." The old man cleared his throat. He pulled a hankie from his pocket and blew his nose with a mighty blast.

"Soon, I'll move to an old-age home, and, I'm sorry to say, you can't come along. They don't allow dogs there, you know." Bent over from age, the old man limped over to Monsieur DuPree and stroked the dog's head.

"Don't worry, my friend. We'll find a home. We'll find a nice new home for you." As an afterthought he added, "Why, with your good looks, we'll have no trouble at all. Anyone would be proud to own such a fine dog."

Monsieur DuPree wagged his tail really hard and strutted up and down the kitchen floor. For a moment, the familiar musky scent of the old man mingling with the odor of greasy food gave the dog a feeling of well-being. But then a sense of dread took hold again. His tail hung between his legs and he stood very still.

"Come here." With great difficulty, the old man knelt down on the floor and lovingly pulled Monsieur DuPree close to him. He tied a ribbon around the dog's neck with a huge red bow, and then he attached a note to it. *What does it say?* Monsieur DuPree wondered.

"It says," the old man read aloud, "Merry Christmas! My name is Monsieur DuPree. For breakfast, I like bacon and eggs—even cornflakes will do. For dinner, I prefer mashed potatoes and some meat. That's all. I eat just two meals a day. In return, I will be your most loyal friend."

"Woof, woof! Woof, woof!" Monsieur DuPree was confused, and his eyes begged, *What's going on?*

The old man blew his nose into his hankie once more. Then, hanging on to a chair, he pulled himself up from the floor. He buttoned his overcoat, reached for the dog's leash and softly said, "Come here, my friend." He opened the door against a gust of cold air and stepped outside, pulling the dog behind. Dusk was beginning to fall. Monsieur DuPree pulled back. He didn't want to go.

"Don't make this any harder for me. I promise you, you'll be much better off with someone else."

The street was deserted. Leaning into the wintry air, the old man and his dog pushed on. It began to snow.

After a very long time, they came upon an old Victorian house surrounded by tall trees, which were swaying and humming in the wind. Shivering in the cold, they appraised the house. Glimmering lights adorned every window, and the muffled sound of a Christmas song was carried on the wind.

"This will be a nice home for you," the old man said, choking on his words. He bent down and unleashed his dog, then opened the gate slowly, so that it wouldn't creak. "Go on now. Go up the steps and scratch on the door."

Monsieur DuPree looked from the house to his master and back again to the house. He did not understand. *"Woof, woof! Woof, woof!"*

Monsieur DuPree was hurt. He thought his master didn't love him anymore. He didn't understand that, indeed, the old man loved him very much but could no longer care for him. Slowly, the dog straggled toward the house and up the steps. He scratched with one paw at the front door. *"Woof, woof! Woof, woof!"*

Looking back, he saw his master step behind a tree just as someone from inside turned the doorknob. A little boy appeared, framed in the doorway by the warm light coming from within. When he saw Monsieur DuPree, the little boy threw both arms into the air and shouted with delight, "Oh, boy! Mom and Dad, come see what Santa brought!"

Through teary eyes, the old man watched from behind the tree as the boy's mother read the note. Then she tenderly pulled Monsieur DuPree inside. Smiling, the old man wiped his eyes with the sleeve of his cold, damp coat. Then he disappeared into the night, whispering, "Merry Christmas, my friend."

Christa Holder Ocker

Christa Holder Ocker is a poet and author for all seasons with a special interest in rhyming picture book stories. A frequent contributor to the Chicken Soup books, her story "Merry Christmas, My Friend," appeared on television, starring Mickey Rooney.

Santa's Secret

Let us think about each other and help each other to show love and do good deeds.

Hebrews 10:24

One weekend, Henry Ford's grandson came to him and said, "Granddaddy, I don't believe in Santa Claus anymore. I think he's a phony."

Mr. Henry, startled by the statement, thought to himself for a moment before answering. What can I do? He's probably heard the older boys at school laugh at anyone who said they believed in Santa Claus. He doesn't want to be laughed at. I'll work on this.

"Well," he finally answered, "let's see what happens this Christmas before coming to a final conclusion about ol' Santa."

Three managers at the Ford Motor Company became Santa Claus consultants to their boss during the next week. The problem: How does an adult prove to a child that Santa Claus exists?

By the end of the week, a plan fell into place. A circus, based in Michigan, headed south for warmer temperatures and their winter tour. Some members stayed in Michigan and had other jobs during the cold months. One of these was a skilled carpenter who carved toys.

Learning about the man, Mr. Ford offered him the job of being Santa's helper. The carpenter accepted the job; dependable income meant he didn't have to spend time hawking his toys from store to store.

A small cabin in the midst of several acres of forest outside Dearborn served as the workshop site. For several weeks, the carpenter set about the tasks of a toymaker. Purchase of a Santa suit, and a long, white costume beard gave traditional authenticity to the busy toymaker.

Nature cooperated fully. A week before Christmas Day, an eight-inch snowfall covered the woods. Reindeer, brought in for the occasion, foraged in the underbrush. A Christmas card artist could not have improved the setting.

As Henry Ford's driver, I got a call from Mr. Ford. "Woody, bring my car by the office. I want you to take my grandson and me for a ride in the woods." I sensed I was in for a noteworthy experience with the automobile magnate.

Once underway, I was directed to an old logging road that led to the toymaker cabin. Finally, we arrived in a small clearing. Light reached out through the cabin windows,

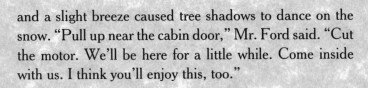

and a slight breeze caused tree shadows to dance on the snow. "Pull up near the cabin door," Mr. Ford said. "Cut the motor. We'll be here for a little while. Come inside with us. I think you'll enjoy this, too."

We knocked and entered the cabin. The red-and-white-suited carpenter appeared to be busy at work. The wide-eyed grandson looked around the shop in disbelief. One after another, he began to examine each toy. The pleased granddad said, "Let me know the toys you like best and maybe Santa will bring them to you for Christmas." Ford followed the boy around the shop and listened to his excited comments. We were all enchanted as we savored the imagination of "Once upon a time . . ."

The tour ended at the workbench of the busy carpenter. A dozen questions poured forth from the inquisitive boy. One after another, the questions were answered from tradition and the imagination of the toymaker. He, too, had inquisitive children.

On leaving, we wished Santa's helper a very Merry Christmas. But this was not the end of the story. Henry Ford didn't forget what pleasure the event had brought to his grandson—or to himself. In subsequent Christmas seasons, hundreds of smiling children journeyed into the woods near Dearborn, Michigan to discover Santa's workshop. Each one received a hand-carved toy from Santa's helper.

The happy children never knew the name of their benefactor. It was Santa's secret.

Woody McKay, Jr.

(This first person account took place when the author's father—also known as Woody—worked for Henry Ford from 1914-1918.)

Woody McKay, Jr., a retired minister, grew up listening to tales about Henry Ford. His father, also called Woody, had been the personal associate of the auto magnate for several years before entering WWI in 1918. Selected anecdotes have been expanded by his son and appeared in Antique Automobile magazine. He lives in Georgia with his wife and over a dozen grandchildren nearby.

23

The Christmas Nandina

*Difficult times have helped me to understand better
than before how infinitely rich and beautiful life is in
every way and that so many things that one goes wor-
rying about are of no importance whatsoever.*

Isak Dinesen

Anne and Paul had their first marital spat on
December 15, three months after the wedding.
Anne had been making exquisite lace orna-
ments for weeks and now she wanted to buy their first
Christmas tree, a special tree, one they would always
remember.

"But we already have our Christmas tree," Paul told her,
and he went to the patio to get the nandina bush.

"A bush?" she asked, laughing, believing he must be teasing her. "A bush in a black plastic pot?"

But Paul was not teasing.

"The Norberts always have a nandina bush at Christmas. I guess I should have told you sooner, but it never occurred to me because it's just something we've done since I was twelve years old. It's our holiday tradition now and I won't change it."

Her face flushed. Oh, the nandina bush was pretty in its own way. It had been out on their patio since after their wedding when Paul had moved his things from the apartment he shared with his two brothers. Pretty as it was, though, it was not a Christmas tree. It was not something she wanted to place her lovely handmade ornaments on, and it would hardly hold even one string of the tiny white lights.

"But why?"

"Listen, Anne," he said. "Dad died when Davey was two years old, and Mom did her best for the next three years. Then she got sick."

Anne listened as he went on to explain that his mother, Julia, had lost so many hours at the hosiery mill due to her illness that what little she had been able to provide for her three sons deteriorated rapidly. Mounting medical bills took priority as she tried desperately to get well.

"That was the first year we did not have a Christmas tree," Paul said, holding her close. "Randy was eight, Davey was five, and I was twelve—and disgusted. I wanted a Christmas tree. All my friends had one, and I was angry that we couldn't have one, too."

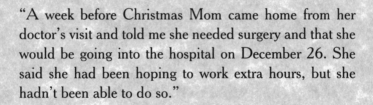

"A week before Christmas Mom came home from her doctor's visit and told me she needed surgery and that she would be going into the hospital on December 26. She said she had been hoping to work extra hours, but she hadn't been able to do so."

"I'm going to need your help, Paul, to make Christmas special this year," she had told her oldest son.

Resentfully, Paul had listened to his mother's idea and helped her dig up the nandina bush from the yard and put it in a black plastic pot.

"I've always loved nandinas," she had said. "My grand-mother had nandinas in her yard back in North Carolina and there were always lovely red berries at Christmastime. See how many berries there are? They'll show up pretty if you and the boys put a few ornaments on it."

Paul thought of the tall trees with glittering ornaments and stars his friends had described, and the nandina bush seemed a poor substitute.

"We tried to decorate it to look like a real Christmas tree, and Randy and Davey thought it was great fun. Davey was too young to remember the Christmas trees we had in the past, and Randy was always good-natured and eager to please so he didn't even question this strange substitute. No. I was the only one who hated the thing."

Julia had made it clear she understood Paul's anger and dis-appointment but she went on with her arrangements—

packing a small bag for the hospital and trying to prepare food for them to have until she could get back home.

"On Christmas Eve morning we all walked the six blocks to church with us boys fussing when we had to stop several times to let Mom rest. When we finally reached the gray stone steps, she told me to stay outside with my brothers until she came back.

"After a while I began to get anxious. People were arriving for the special children's service and to see the living nativity on the church lawn.

"My brothers were restless and started arguing, and I was worried that we would be late for the service. Besides, I was angry that I had been left outside with them so I went to find Mom."

Paul had wandered through the halls until he heard his mother's voice, talking softly and crying. It was something he had never seen his mother do.

". . . and—well, if anything happens to me, my boys . . ."

Paul's heart pounded as he stood listening.

"My oldest one, Paul—well, he's had to help me so much since I've been sick. I really . . ."

"It wasn't until then that I knew Mom was much sicker than I had realized and that she was very worried about us. I slipped back outside and told the boys that I couldn't find her. When she came out, she was smiling. Randy and Davey didn't even notice that her face was swollen and her eyes still teary, and we all went inside to the children's Christmas Eve service as if nothing were wrong.

"I had no idea when they were delivered, but the next morning there had been several gifts piled on the table by the nandina bush. One for each of us from Mom and the others from our friends at church.

"There were two gifts for me," Paul said, smiling at the memory. "A Scrabble game and a book—a Hardy Boys mystery. I still have them."

Julia had lain on the sofa, all smiles, as the little boys screeched in the delight of ripping the bright wrapping paper. She had made their favorite breakfast—hot chocolate and monkey bread.

"Later in the morning, Randy's Sunday school teacher brought a huge tray of turkey, dressing, and a bag of other good things we had not eaten for a very long time. After Randy and Davey went to bed that night, Mom gave me pen and paper and asked me to write a thank-you note to our church who had provided for us on such short notice when she had been unable to do so herself.

"Mom went to sleep lying on the sofa, watching the tiny lights twinkle on the nandina bush while I sat at the kitchen table rewriting the thank-you note she had dictated so that it would be neat as she insisted.

"The next day she went to the hospital and she never came home. That was the first Christmas 'tree' that Davey would remember, and it was the last one we had with Mom. We came to North Carolina to live with Aunt Violet, who loved us and helped us through that first lonely, frightening year. Most of all she understood why, the following Christmas, we insisted on decorating the nandina bush we had brought from home.

"I love you, Anne, but in this one thing I won't give in."

Anne nodded, unable to speak, now seeing beyond the simple little bush to the love of a mother long departed who had left three sons behind, each possessing her quiet strength and tenderness. Julia had bequeathed to them a legacy of love, which now included Anne, and would include the children of Paul and Anne who were yet to come; children with whom they would share each year the story of the Christmas nandina.

Elizabeth Silance Ballard

Elizabeth Silance Ballard is a writer and social worker whose short stories have appeared in magazines and anthologies since 1975. Her book, Three Letters From Teddy and Other Stories, *contains more stories we know you will enjoy. She can be reached at P.O. Box 9105, Virginia Beach, VA 23450 or by E-mail at elizsilbal@aol.com.*

Celebrating Ben

Love never dies as long as there is someone who remembers.

Leo Buscaglia

"**Y**ou get like this every year," my husband said in exasperation last November, sitting on the bed where I lay teary-eyed. "I do everything I can think of to make you feel better, but nothing works. Christmas is no fun for either of us anymore. Is it always going to be this way?" When I didn't reply, he left the room.

In my misery, I thought, *He simply doesn't understand.* However, if anyone understood, it was Jay. But he couldn't make Christmas okay for me. No one could.

In 1986, Ben, my ten-year-old son—the stepson Jay had loved deeply for seven years—was hit by a car and killed. I had hated the holidays ever since. While I missed Ben every day, his loss was keenest at this time of year, with its emphasis on celebration, joy, and family togetherness. For years after Ben's death, I went through the motions of a happy Christmas for the sake of our other three children. I kept my spirits up for them while grieving in private for their younger brother. But now that our daughters were grown and lived away from home, my holiday depression had resurfaced with a vengeance. I wanted to turn back time. I wanted my little boy back so we could experience the wonder and joy of Christmas again—the way it was before our family was plunged into anguish by a tragic moment on a busy street.

As I wrestled with my feelings, I realized that I didn't want to ruin another holiday season for Jay. I owed him more than that. But did I even have it within me to feel the spirit of Christmas once again?

One evening several days later, I was talking to one of my daughters over the phone when I mentioned how much Ben had been on my mind. For a moment, there was silence. Then she spoke, her voice breaking with emotion, "I've been thinking about him, too. Ever since he died, I've just wanted to get Christmas over with."

Her words jolted me. All those years, I thought the girls were having a good time celebrating the holidays. Had they been putting on an act for my sake? Had they, too, become incapable of enjoying what I knew deep in my heart could be the happiest, best time of year?

I had thought that somehow, as the years passed, I would naturally begin to anticipate the holiday season again. As I hung up the phone, I realized that time couldn't make this happen; Ben would always be missing from our lives, and we would always feel his loss most acutely at this time of year. But if I could acknowledge my grief instead of stifling it, and honor my son's memory at the same time, perhaps I could find joy in the holidays again—which meant Jay could, too. Then we might be able to help our daughters rekindle their own Christmas spirit.

I told Jay that I didn't want to spend December under a cloud of gloom. He offered to do whatever he could to help me, and we came up with a plan. First, we would work at finding pleasure in all that was magical and wonderful about the holidays. Second, we would speak of Ben whenever he came to mind—no holding back for fear of depressing ourselves or others. Finally, we would do one special thing to commemorate how much we missed our son. All three, it turned out, were important.

Starting with the first goal, I concentrated on engaging my senses to the fullest. For the past ten years, I had shut them down, numbing myself to the twinkle of lights, the sound of carols, the smell of evergreen, the tastes of mint, almond and ginger. Now, I embraced them. I also gave more thought to each holiday task—from wrapping presents to mailing cards—appreciating them as time-honored rituals instead of dreary chores to get out of the way.

I unpacked several paper-and-paste ornaments Ben had made in grade school, including a primitive little yarn frame with his school picture in it. Closing my eyes, I ran

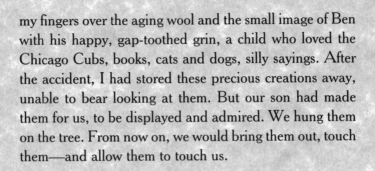

my fingers over the aging wool and the small image of Ben with his happy, gap-toothed grin, a child who loved the Chicago Cubs, books, cats and dogs, silly sayings. After the accident, I had stored these precious creations away, unable to bear looking at them. But our son had made them for us, to be displayed and admired. We hung them on the tree. From now on, we would bring them out, touch them—and allow them to touch us.

Several weeks before Christmas, I had lunch with an old friend I had not seen for many months. She dwelled at length on how much she hated the holidays—too much rich food, too many expectations. Then she lamented feeling "deserted" because her newly married son would be spending the holidays with his wife's family.

The old me would have nodded while inwardly screaming, "At least you *have* your son. Look at me—your pain is *nothing* compared to mine!" But I had vowed not to keep quiet when Ben was on my mind. I took a deep breath and forced myself to sympathize with her. Then, measuring my words carefully, I told her that I was trying hard to enjoy the holidays in spite of how much I still missed Ben.

My friend looked startled, and for a moment I regretted saying anything. Then she put her hand on my arm. Her eyes were moist. "I think this is the first time since Ben's death that you've mentioned him to me," she said. "Whenever I started to say something about him, I could tell you didn't want to talk about it . . . but now I know . . ." Her words caught in her throat. "You've just given me a special gift. I'm going to be grateful for what I have and stop complaining."

I nevertheless would have given anything to be able to commiserate, but at least I had finally spoken. And in breaking my silence at long last, I let my friend draw me close.

A few days later, while shopping, Jay and I stopped in a busy department store café for espresso. There, I was suddenly reminded of one Christmas we had spent nursing Ben through the flu. As I recalled this to Jay, tears welled in his eyes, then in mine. "I miss him so much," he whispered. There, amid the bustle of holiday shoppers, we held hands under the table, let our tears fall, and managed to smile at each other, enriched by our shared remembrance and our love.

We were discussing how best to accomplish our third goal of honoring Ben's memory when we saw a notice in the local newspaper about "A Service of Remembrance: In Memory of Those We Miss the Most at Christmas." Jay and I didn't belong to that church or its denomination, but no matter. We gathered with a hundred other bereaved souls, and in a candlelight service we listened to comforting words and beautiful music, including the haunting song "I Miss You Most at Christmastime." Then we put the names of the people we had loved and lost into a special basket on the altar.

My tears felt especially healing that night, and I entered the busy final week before Christmas with a sense of peace that had eluded me in years past. Over the phone, we shared our feelings with our daughters and listened as they expressed their own sadness about Ben. When we wished them Merry Christmas, I felt we all could truly have one at last.

Christmas would never be what it was, but it could still be good.

And this, I knew, was what Ben would want for us.

Andrea Warren

Andrea Warren, an award-winning author, is best known for her historical non-fiction books for young readers, including Orphan Train Rider: One Boy's True Story, We Rode the Orphan Trains, Pioneer Girl: Growing Up on the Prairie, *and* Surviving Hitler: A Boy in the Nazi Death Camps. *Her website is AndreaWarren.com.*

Hold Christmas Fast

Hold Christmas fast, oh one and all,
Children, elders, great and small,
With merry wreaths on memory's wall
Keep Christmas in the hearts of all!

Hold Christmas fast so that its light
Makes every street more safely bright
Till goodwill conquers hate's dark night
And all the world is cleansed with light!

Let Christmas live, its gladness ring
Sweet as the songs the angels sing;
To everyone and everything
Its story and its glory bring!

Keep Christmas near, yes, make it last
Long after this short season's past,
Till faith survives fear's wintry blast
And love's fair summer reigns at last!

Make Christmas last, and let it be
The telescope through which we see
God's promise of Eternity
Beyond our brief mortality!

John C. Bonser

John C. Bonser is a retired businessman, past president of St. Louis County Community Chamber of Commerce and The Rotary Club of Overland, Missouri. His award-winning poetry has appeared in numerous publications. John and his wife, Betty, reside at Triangle Apts., 1200 Traingle Dr., St. Peters, Missouri, 63033.

A Light in the Window

Heaven's light forever shines. . .
Percy Bysshe Shelley

I love Christmas traditions! One of my favorites is the placing of lights in windows, for it reminds me of a beautiful story I have heard different people tell over the years about John Todd, a very distinguished individual who earned his place in history long ago. As a small boy, he was only six years old when his father and mother died. Soon after he was orphaned and left all alone, he received a letter from his aunt who lived a long distance away. He had never met her, but she wrote, *"John, come live with me. I'm your aunt. I love you. I'll be your mother and father."*

So instead of going to an orphanage, he went to live with his aunt. Because she was wealthy, she gave him advantages he never would have had. John attended the university, and then moved away to attain a theological education. He worked hard and distinguished himself as a clergyman. One day when he was forty-one years old, he received a letter from his aunt that said, *"John, you know I don't write a letter unless it's important . . . so you know this is important."* She continued, *"The doctor tells me I have a terminal illness and shall soon die. John, I'm no scholar like you. What do you think I can expect?"*

John wrote back to his aunt, and his letter has become a classic piece of literature. The letter is entitled:

"The Letter of a Little Boy of Six,
Written 35 Years Later."

Dear Auntie,

It is now thirty-five years since I, a little boy of six, was left alone in the world. You sent me word that you would give me a home and be a kind mother to me. I've never forgotten the day when I made that long journey to your house. I can still recall my disappointment when I learned that instead of coming for me yourself, you sent your hired man to fetch me. I can still remember my tears as, perched on a horse, I clung tightly to the back of your hired man, and we started trotting off to my new home.

Night fell before we finished the journey. As the darkness deepened, I began to be afraid. I said to the man in front of me, "Do you think she'll go to bed before I get there?" And he said, throwing his head back to me as the horse trotted on, "Oh no. She'll surely stay up for you, Johnny. When we get out of these woods, you'll see her candle lighted up presently."

As we rode into a clearing, there, sure enough, I did see a friendly candle in the window. I remember that you were waiting in the door. You put your arms around me, a tired, frightened little lad, and lifted me down from the horse.

I remember there was a bright fire with a hearth and a warm supper on the stove. After supper you took me up to my room and heard me say my prayers. Then you sat beside me until I fell asleep. You're probably wondering why I'm recalling all of this now, Auntie. Well, your letter reminded me of it. For one day soon, God will send for you to take you to your new home. Don't fear the summons, or the strange journey, or the messenger. At the end of the road, you'll see a light in the window, and standing in the doorway, smiling to welcome you will be Jesus. You will be safe forevermore. Auntie, God can be trusted to be as kind to you as you were to me thirty-five years ago.

Love,

John

Every time I read John Todd's words, I imagine his aunt reading those same words and breathing a deep sigh of comfort, becoming completely enveloped in a divine peace, as if in a warm, soft blanket. As I grow older, this story grows more and more precious to me, too. I can breathe a sigh of assurance. I know my days will someday come to an end, and when they do, God will send for me. And waiting for me will be the most precious Christmas gift I've ever received, a new home in heaven—"with a bright fire in the hearth and a warm supper on the stove."

As retold by Barbara Chesser

115

A Special Invitation

You have a special invitation to submit true stories you would like to share with others in future editions of Keeping Christmas. *Please send favorite stories, serious or humorous, you have read or stories you have written to:*

Dr. Barbara Chesser
2617 Regency
Waco, TX 76710

or

ChristmasStories@hot.rr.com

About Barbara Chesser

Barbara Chesser, Ph.D. grew up hearing the deep rich chords of storytelling. As a child, she enjoyed her large extended family's heartwarming stories, and that family tradition is still very much alive today—especially on holidays like Christmas.

Barbara has taught at several universities, and her work has taken her to Greece, the Philippines, and the African countries of Nigeria, Tanzania, Swaziland, and Morocco. Graduating at the top of her university class, Barbara continues her pursuit of excellence with a "human touch," including the compilation of *Keeping Christmas*. Barbara has received numerous awards for outstanding university teaching, research, and writing.

Co-authored books include *Chicken Soup for the Golden Soul*, one of the most popular books in the Chicken Soup series; it has appeared on all the major best-seller lists and is approaching one million copies sold. Barbara also co-authored a marriage and family college textbook and three other books and is the sole author of several other award-winning books. Barbara has also written for professional journals and popular magazines, including the *Journal of Religion and Health* and *Reader's Digest*.

For the past twelve years Barbara has served as president of The Meyer Resource Group, Inc., a research and development company in a global enterprise serving affiliated companies throughout the United States and in twenty-two languages in more than sixty countries throughout the world.

Barbara's home life centers on Del, Christi, Michael, and Jackson. Dr. Del Chesser is Barbara's husband, a Baylor University professor and a CPA. Christi is their daughter; she is also a CPA. Michael is Christi's husband and is a computer programmer. As the newest member of the family, Jackson is Christi and Michael's son and Del and Barbara's grandson. Jackson is the family expert on "keeping Christmas," for he fills every day with love and joy.